a
ah! oh!

Example: A! (Oh!)

akesi

non-cute animal, reptile

Example: akesi li tawa lon ma. (The reptile is moving on the ground.)

ala

no, not, none, zero

Example: mi wile ala e ni. (I don't want that.)

alasa

to hunt, gather, search for

Example: mi alasa e kili. (I am gathering fruit.)

ale

everything, all, life, the universe

Example: ale li pona. (Everything is good.)

ali

everything, everyone, life, the universe

Example: ali li jo e suno. (Everyone has the sun.)

anpa

bottom, lower part, to bow down

Example: mi tawa anpa. (I am going down.)

ante
different, other, change, alter

Example: tomo ante li lon poka mi. (A different house is next to mine.)

anu

or (used between options)

Example: mi lon tomo anu tomo sina. (I am at your place or his/her place.)

awen

to stay, wait, remain, keep

Example: mi awen lon tomo. (I am staying in the house.)

e

marks direct object of verb

Example: mi moku e kili.. (I am eating fruit.)

en

and (used between subjects)

Example: mi en sina li pona. (Me and you are good.)

esun

market, shop, buy, trade

Example: mi tawa esun. (I am going to the market.)

ijo

thing, something, stuff, object

Example: tomo li ijo. (A house is a thing.)

ike

bad, negative, wrong, evil

Example: ni li ike. (This is bad.)

ilo

tool, machine, thing to use

Example: mi pana e ilo tawa sina. (I am giving a tool to you.)

insa

inside, stomach, center

Example: tomo mi li lon insa ma. (My house is inside the land.)

jaki

dirty, gross, pollution

Example: tomo mi li jaki. (My house is dirty.)

jan

person, people, someone, anybody

Example: mi jan. (I am a person.)

jelo
yellow, light green

Example: kili jelo li pona tawa mi. (I like yellow fruit.)

jo
have, possess, own

Example: mi jo e palisa. (I have a stick.)

kala
fish, sea creature

Example: kala li lon telo. (Fish are in the water.)

kalama

sound, noise, make noise

Example: mi kalama. (I am making noise.)

kama

to come, happen, event

Example: mi kama. (I am coming.)

kasi
plant, leaf, herb, tree

*Example: mi pana e kasi tawa tomo. (I am
decorating the house with plants.)*

ken

can, is able to, is allowed to

Example: sina ken. (You can.)

kepeken

using, with the help of

Example: mi sitelen kepeken ilo pi sitelen. (I am writing with a pen.)

kijetesantakalu

A procyonid, such as a raccoon, coati, kinkajou, olingo, ringtail, or cacomistle

Example: kijetesantakalu tonsi li lanpan ala lanpan e soko?. (Does the non-binary musteloid steal mushrooms?)

kili

fruit, vegetable

Example: kili li moku. (Fruit is food.)

kin

also, even, indeed

Example: mi kin li tomo ante. (I also have a different house.)

kipisi

to cut, slice, divide

Example: mi kipisi e palisa. (I am cutting the stick.)

kiwen

stone, rock, hard thing

Example: kiwen li suli. (Stones are big.)

ko

semi-solid or squishy substance, e.g., paste, gum

Example: mi pali e ko moku. (I am making food paste.)

kon
air, wind, atmosphere, breath

Example: tomo mi li lon kon. (My house is in the air.)

kule

color, paint, colorful

Example: mi kule e tomo. (I am painting the house.)

kulupu

group, community, society

Example: kulupu mi li pona. (My community is good.)

kute
ear, to hear, listen

Example: mi kute e kalama (I am listening to the sound).

la

(introduces a dependent clause)

Example: mi la, mi tawa. (When I go, I leave.)

lape
sleep, rest, lying down

Example: mi lape. (I am sleeping.)

laso

blue, green

Example: mi kule e kili laso. (I like green fruit.)

lawa

head, mind, control

Example: lawa mi li suli. (My head is big.)

len

clothing, cloth, dress

Example: len sina li pona. (Your clothing is good.)

lete

cold, cool

Example: mi lete. (I am cold.)

li

(separates subject from
predicate)

Example: mi li lon tomo. (I am in the house.)

lili

small, little, a few, a bit

Example: mi jo e tomo lili. (I have a small house.)

linja

long, very thin thing, e.g., string, hair

Example: linja mi li sike. (My hair is curly.)

lipu

flat object, e.g., paper, card, book

Example: mi lukin e lipu. (I am looking at a book.)

loje

red

Example: mi kule e tomo loje. (I am painting a red house.)

lon

be, exist, be there, happen

Example: mi lon. (I am here.)

luka

hand, arm

Example: mi jo e luka (I have a hand)

lukin

eye, to see, look at, watch

Example: mi lukin. (I am looking.)

lupa

hole, orifice, window, door

Example: mi open e lupa. (I am opening a door.)

ma

land, country, earth, outdoor environment

Example: ma li pona. (The land is good.)

mama

parent, creator, source

Example: mama mi li pona. (My parent is good.)

mani

money, material wealth

Example: mi jo e mani. (I have money.)

meli

woman, female

Example: meli li jan. (Women are people.)

mi

I, me, we

Example: mi li jan. (I am a person.)

moku

to eat, food

Example: mi moku e kili. (I am eating fruit.)

moli

death, to die, dead

Example: jan li moli. (People die.)

monsi

back, rear end, behind

Example: mi tomo li lon monsi mi. (My house is behind me.)

musi

art, entertainment, fun

Example: mi musi. (I am having fun.)

mun

moon, celestial body

Example: mun li lon. (The moon is there.)

mute

many, much, more, a lot

Example: jan mute li lon ni. (There are many people here.)

nanpa

number

Example: nanpa mi li luka tu. (My number is five.)

nasa

silly, crazy, foolish

Example: sina nasa. (You are crazy.)

nasin

way, manner, custom

Example: nasin mi li suli. (My path is long.)

nena

bump, hill, mountain

Example: nena li lon tomo mi (There is a hill near my house).

ni

this, that

Example: ni li tomo. (This is a house.)

nimi

word, name

Example: nimi mi li suli. (My name is long.)

noka

foot, leg

Example: mi tawa e noka. (I am moving my foot.)

o

(vocative or imperative marker)

Example: o, sina toki. (Speak, you!)

oko

eye

Example: mi lukin e oko. (I am looking at an eye.)

olin

love, have affection for

Example: mi olin e sina. (I love you.)

ona

he, she, it, they

Example: ona li tomo. (It is a house.)

open
open, start, turn on

Example: mi open e tomo. (I am opening the house.)

pakala

mistake, accident, damage

Example: mi pakala e tomo. (I am damaging the house.)

pali

do, make, build, create

Example: mi pali. (I am working.)

palisa

long, hard object, e.g., rod, stick

Example: mi jo e palisa. (I have a stick.)

pan
grain, cereal, bread

Example: mi moku e pan. (I am eating bread.)

pana

give, send, emit

Example: mi pana e soweli. (I am giving an animal.)

pi
of, belonging to

Example: tomo pi mi. (My house.)

pilin

feeling, emotion, think

Example: mi pilin. (I am feeling.)

pimeja
black, dark

Example: tenpo pimeja li pimeja. (The night is dark.)

pini

end, finish, stop

Example: mi pini. (I am finished.)

pipi
insect

Example: pipi li lon kasi. (Insects are in the plants.)

poka

side, hip, next to

Example: tomo mi li poka tomo sina. (My house is next to your house.)

poki

container, box, bowl, bag

Example: mi open e poki. (I am opening a container.)

pona

good, simple, positive, well

Example: mi pona. (I am good.)

pu

the book 'Toki Pona: The Language of Good'

Example: mi pu. (I am reading the book 'Toki Pona: The Language of Good'.)

sama

same, similar, sibling

Example: mi en sina li sama. (Me and you are the same.)

seli

fire, heat

Example: seli li tomo. (Fire is a house.)

selo

surface, skin, outer layer

Example: selo mi li loje. (My skin is red.)

seme

what, which, who

Example: mi toki e ni: mi wile e seme? (I am saying this: What do I want?)

sewi

high, above, sacred

Example: sewi li suli. (The sky is big.)

sijelo
body, physical state

Example: mi pilin e sijelo mi. (I am feeling my body.)

sike

circle, wheel, ball, coin

Example: sike li kule. (Circles are colorful.)

sin
new, fresh, another

Example: tomo mi li sin. (My house is new.)

sina

you

Example: sina li jan. (You are a person.)

sinpin
front, chest, face

Example: mi lon sinpin tomo. (I am in front of the house.)

sitelen

image, representation, draw, write

Example: mi sitelen e tomo. (I am drawing a house.)

sona

knowledge, wisdom, understanding

Example: mi sona e tomo. (I understand the house.)

soweli

mammal, animal

Example: soweli li lon tomo tawa. (Animals are in the vehicle.)

suli
big, tall, important

Example: soweli li suli. (Animals are big.)

suno

sun, light

Example: suno li suli. (The sun is big.)

supa
horizontal surface, table

Example: mi tawa e supa. (I am moving the table.)

suwi

candy, sweet, cute

Example: mi moku e suwi. (I am eating candy.)

tan
cause, reason, because of

Example: mi tawa tan mi. (I am leaving because of me.)

taso

but, only

Example: mi taso. (I alone.)